MORE

DASH

THAN

CASH

VOGUE

MORE DASH THAN CASH

LINDA WATSON
ROSIE MARTIN

BCA

LONDON · NEW YORK · SYDNEY · TORONTO

Text copyright © 1992 Condé Nast Publications Ltd.

Reprinted 1995

The right of Linda Watson and Rosie Martin to be identified as the authors of this work has been asserted by them in accordance with the Copyright, Designs and Patents Act, 1988.

First published in 1992 by Condé Nast Publications Ltd. an imprint of Random House UK Ltd.
Random House, 20 Vauxhall Bridge Road, London SW1V 2SA

Random House Australia (Pty) Ltd., 20 Alfred Street, Milsons Point, Sydney, New South Wales 2061, Australia

Random Century New Zealand Ltd., 18 Poland Road, Glenfield, Auckland 10, New Zealand

Random Century South Africa (Pty) Ltd., P.O. Box 337, Bergvlei 2012, South Africa

Designed by Write Image Ltd

Picture Research by Shona Wood

Set in Times and Eurostyle by SX Composing Ltd
Origination by Colorlito, Milan
Printed and bound in Italy by Graphicom

A catalogue record for this book is available from the British Library.

ISBN 0 09 177418 7 (cased)
ISBN 0 09 177037 8 (paperback)

CONTENTS

INTRODUCTION

There is much more to looking good than a weighty wallet. The most expensive labels in the world are an unconvincing veneer if they fight with your lifestyle, drown your personality and turn you into a fashion clone. A winning appearance requires imagination, but never loses sight of practicalities. Today, a limited budget is a lame excuse for not making the effort. Women now, more than ever, have the run of a wide field of choices. As High Street stores multiply, they compete for our attention by interpreting high fashion and using their ingenuity to explore new territory. It's up to you to pick out the best.

This book is not a directory—it won't point the finger at clothes you should rush out and buy, nor will it tell you *what* to wear *when*. Its aim is to untangle the web, hand you the ammunition—the knowledge—so you can tell at a glance what will last or fall apart, what you'll wear and wear and what's doomed to be a one-season wonder. Fashion is a roller-coaster ride of changes, but some rules last for ever. The right height of heel will always update proportions, for example; good grooming is a constant prerequisite; quality is eternal; certain shapes will maximise your figure type, others will kill it dead.

Outdated concepts may have to fall by the wayside. Extracting maximum mileage from a limited number of clothes means viewing them with an unbiased eye. Be ready to rethink your approach towards colour, to look at pieces from a fresh angle, to merge new ideas with your taste level. The key is to understand when it's worth spending more. If you develop a well-planned, non-obsessive strategy, dressing well becomes second nature.

Great clothes are unobtrusive, but have the power to make a world of difference. The boost to your confidence is uncalculable—you exude enthusiasm, even make it clear you're on the ball. *More Dash Than Cash* demystifies fashion, takes you through your paces and allows you to take control. Enjoy it, you're in the driving seat.

HOT OFF THE PRESS

A quiet word in the ear of sloppy dressers: fashion *is* important. You ask why? Basically, nothing speaks louder about your state of mind than clothes, hair and make-up that are out of sync with the times. Ex-students who, years after the last exam, still live in shabby sweaters and floppy jeans are sending out signals that say they're not ready to go forward on their own; sticking with a hairstyle and make-up format that are relics of a confidence peak warns that a woman has reached a plateau where ambitions can get pushed to one side. If you're not on top of the latest looks, chances are you've switched off from the rest of the world—the current issues, its key players: 'Fashion is like a television screen on the world,' says designer Christian Lacroix, 'made up of all the present trends—music, painting, news, etc.' The trick is knowing how to keep it switched on.

Left *You wouldn't wear it to the office – but you can pick up on the skirt length, the weight of the shoes and rush out to buy a gingham skirt.*

'If a woman is poorly dressed
you notice the clothes. If she is
impeccably dressed, you
notice the woman.'
COCO CHANEL

Being fashionable isn't difficult. You don't have to be extreme or copy every runway shenanigan that makes headlines in fashion capitals. Only fashion victims lift whole looks from a designer's cutting table and indiscriminately pile on fashionable labels. These are the markings of a woman who lacks confidence, let alone imagination. Clothes are a way of defining yourself rather than a mechanism to push you into the mainstream. A far more intelligent approach is to pursue a personal sense of style that includes fashion elements; that means knowing about the big stories and the details—the silhouette, proportions, fabrics, colours, accessories, when to change your hair or height of shoe—and linking them to a basic working wardrobe in ways all your own.

Style bears the hallmarks of your personality. It's a timeless, constant quality that draws you to a way of dressing you feel comfortable with. Some people are born with instinctive good style: they share a common ground in not being overdressed, and are not just clothes hangers for outrageous fashions, but have a special, unforced identity with which they are obviously at ease. The trick is knowing what is right for you. Clothes you battle with and that make you self-conscious destroy any hope of style. 'You should wear your clothes, not let the clothes wear you,' warns British designer Betty Jackson. Good style is not something you can copy—clothes that you admire on someone else won't necessarily be a success for you—but it can be developed with practice, a will to experiment and an honest assessment of your personality and way of life. Think long and hard about how you want to be perceived, your lifestyle and to a lesser extent your shape and age. How you mix colours and textures, the extent you accessorise, the complexity or simplicity of the complete look, personal items—maybe pieces of antique clothing, hats, ethnic jewellery or fabric you've bought abroad—will stamp your distinguishing marks and if you don't see them on anyone else that's good news, not a reason to think they're not *de rigueur*. Step out of the mould: going with the flow like everyone else is safe but mediocre, and witness the boost to your self-esteem.

Originality means constantly viewing clothes from a new angle. This is why fashion with its perpetual motion, its novelty, fun and rejection of anything ordinary, is such a potent, educative medium. Sometimes its movements are lit up in lights, often it works in more subtle ways. For instance, you may have picked up on the new length of skirt, but are you clear what can make it look really new—the right jacket, fabrics, colours, attitude and occasion? The emphasis is on being well informed.

NOT JUST PRETTY PICTURES

Nobody said an inspired appearance wouldn't require effort. Although a limited budget in no way precludes you from looking good—as this book will illustrate—it does impose three necessities: motivation, knowledge and innovation. The medium that ignites all these is a quality, glossy fashion magazine. By bringing together the best photographers, models, locations, writers, editors and designers, a good magazine creates such a glamorous visual image the reader starts to dream. It's that dreaming that sets you thinking, gets you excited about fashion so you treat it as a subject worth working on.

Communicating information is a magazine's *raison d'être*. Although your bank balance may stop you filling your wardrobe with the expensive labels you see in its pages, an understanding of fashion must start with a publication that deals predominantly with the most influential designers. The trouble with magazines that report only mass-market fashion is that you're really seeing diluted versions of ideas that the designer giants came up with anything up to a year previously.

Above *Fashion photography knocks you off balance so you're ready to accept something new. The accessories are unwearable, the clothes are not central to the picture, but the reader can be inspired by a romantic theme that role plays with medievalism, principal-boy swagger and huntress jackets and boots.*

Designers at the top end of fashion are there for a reason—their ability to invent—and it is their concepts that eventually trickle down to the High Street. Magazines at the cutting edge of fashion are privy to the ready-to-wear collections in Milan, Paris, London and New York, which occur in March (the next autumn/winter clothes) and October (spring/summer), and in *Vogue*'s case are reported usually in the August and February issues respectively. Even if you are not a regular magazine buff, these are the issues most worth investing in, so you learn about designs several months before they appear in the shops. The difficulty is drumming up enough enthusiasm for, say, winter clothes in August when they hit the news stands, but it's important to 'get an eye in' ahead of time because knowing what's coming in winter will influence what you buy for summer. Plus, you're in a position to use some of the details, themes and colours early; if you wait till fashion trends hit the High Street, as far as fashion experts are concerned, they are already out of date.

On the surface, the haute couture collections that *Vogue* records in April and October may have little relevance to your wardrobe at home. The prices involved are huge and middle-market labels can never hope to mirror the couturier's lavish beading, time-consuming intricacies and cutting expertise. However, traditionally, it is inside the cloistered buildings of haute couture houses that designers are pushed to their creative limits, unbridled by factors that constrict them in ready-to-wear, such as wearability, fabrics, time and cost. Here the seeds of many fashion trends are sown, which filter down through the ready-to-wear and ultimately into cheaper brands. In recent seasons, a natural raffia/straw/wicker element threaded through haute couture, which was easily interpreted with very little expense. How wonderful to be handed the chance to lead the way.

The sheer volume of images streaming out from the runways can be confusing, but a good magazine editor will edit them into coherent trends and sift out the gimmicks, leaving only the directional fashion. Throughout the season, the magazine's intention is to offer variables, showing how the runways can be worked to their maximum potential. The advantage fashion editors have is that they see the whole fashion market—from the established, respected names to the newest designer with the first flickers of talent. You should see the flurry of activity in the fashion room at *Vogue*: rails upon rails of clothes, with fashion editors and their assistants experimenting with accessories, mixing labels, trying on clothes to assess the way they hang, deciphering which are the most perfectly shaped trousers, coats, shirts, etc.

HIGH FASHION TO HIGH STREET: HOW IT WORKS

Between *Vogue* running the photograph on the left and the other two, there are thirteen months—the time it takes for fashion to travel from runway to High Street. (left) This look, which draws inspiration from the life and times of Forties gangsters Bonnie and Clyde, was an innovative image, not just because of the getaway car and mock sub-machine gun, but because of the John Galliano suit. It was new for two reasons: firstly, mannish pinstripes were being worn by a woman; secondly, the skirt was long and had a split that revealed a good deal of leg. The tough sexiness of a moll provided the mood. Just over a year later the look hit the High Street. It was simpler, less theatrical, but picked up on the mood and core elements of the original and presented them in a wearable form: (centre) a pinstripe shorts suit; (right) an ankle-length skirt that shows the leg, topped with a man's jacket; both worn with that heavy dose of sex appeal.

This process is akin to concentrated shopping and saves the reader time by handing her the best shapes and colours on a plate. The pieces that pass the test are hurriedly packed into bulging suitcases and taken to be photographed. On the shoot, the editor starts to improvise: tying a shirt in a new way; using a scarf or piece of antique fabric as a skirt; juxtaposing colours to create a surprise; mixing evening accessories with day wear. One fashion editor is infamous for telling a model to slip her legs through the arms of a cardigan and wear it as a pair of trousers. Magazines teach you to adjust your ideas of what's appropriate: 'If you see a shot of a denim shirt worn with a ballroom skirt, don't say how ridiculous; think if denim can penetrate even evening wear, it's clearly an important thread through the collections,' advises Harrods's fashion consultant, Vanessa de Lisle. The photographer, editor, hair and make-up artist have a theme in mind and are interpreting it in the most original evocative way they know. 'Give 'em [the readers] what they never knew they wanted!' was the brief American *Vogue*'s great former editor, Diana Vreeland, once gave her fashion editors: if the magazine's doing its job well you won't see what you expect to find.

Open its pages with an open mind—don't dismiss obscure pictures out of hand—look at extremes and try to understand them. The swashbuckling fencer on page 125, wearing slicked hair, an eye patch, a steely glare, bustier, tight leggings, silver beads and buckled shoes is a role model that would no doubt be viewed with some scepticism if imitated at the office, but no matter: *Vogue* isn't dictating, it's telling you about fashion's new moods, colours and points of emphasis. In the case of the fencer, she is an icon for fashion's one-time preoccupation with body-conscious clothes, metallics and cavalier flamboyancy, but how you adapt these ideas—not necessarily the actual clothes—is left to you. The purpose of the photograph is to nudge you off balance, knock you out of a groove, so you're ready to accept change, and sometimes the only image that does the job is a strong one.

WHERE READERS GO WRONG

Whilst magazine glossies are powerful vehicles for escapism, dreams have to be kept in check. It's no good going into a trance about sunny distant shores, the glamorous lifestyles of the rich and famous, the long-legged figures of models in perfect clothes, and ending up feeling dissatisfied with your lot. Chances are then you'll throw the magazine away, frustrated that it never shows clothes you can afford and fashion becomes a dirty word for good. Keep your feet on the ground and remember that if magazines do show some clothes whose prices seem inexplicably high, it's not through any malicious intention to torment the reader, but because the best fashion features are usually found in expensive lines. No one is asking you to rush out and buy all the clothes in fashion pages; magazines serve to show fashion's direction, they are never intended to be just catalogues. Even if the prices *were* lower, you can't lift a whole look from a page and put it on yourself. Firstly, you are probably physically different from the model in proportions and colouring. Secondly, your environment is not the same. Thirdly, you shouldn't be emulating others—you should be the person they turn to for inspiration!

HOW YOU SHOULD USE A MAGAZINE

Absorbing fashion is like osmosis: it comes gradually to anyone who's willing to let it in. The more images you see, the more quickly you'll become sensitive to its nuances.

• Dissect the fashion pages with a toothcomb. Circle what you like, cut pages out, even compile a scrapbook.

• Points to look for: proportions, themes, colours, fabrics and accessories. It is fashion's intrinsic peculiarity that designers work independently of one another, yet more times than not are united in their directions for the season. New themes may carry the distinguishing marks of each designer, but amongst the trees you can see the common wood. Work out whether the dominant shape is essentially narrow, like a vertical line, or marks out an upright inverted triangle. Is the weight on top or below, or is it evenly distributed? Have the designers looked to a common source for inspiration? Is the source something you could expand on? If the shapes are similar to those of previous seasons, try to distinguish what has been changed to make the look new.

• Questions to ask yourself: Where is the focus? Is the waist accentuated? What length is the skirt? How long is the jacket? Where does it cut the skirt? Are the legs a feature? Is the bust important? How high and heavy are the heels? Why, when fashion editors have so much to choose from, have they selected that particular jacket or skirt? What does it have in common with the rest of the pieces in the story? What is the hair doing? Has the make-up changed?

• Look beyond the main stories to the subtleties. For example, a simple slip dress might come through strongly but the precise scoop of its neckline could make the difference between one that makes it and one that just misses.

• Pick up a mood from a fashion story. Even when the clothes are not shown as clearly as you would wish, look at the lighting, the location, the attitude of the model—is it film-star glamour, energetic or feminine? The clothes may be expensive, but a mood can be created on any budget with make-up, the right fabrics and colours. A photograph is not a haphazard affair, it's designed to tell the reader as much as possible. For example, black-and-white film may indicate when important shapes, not colours, are being introduced. A Chanel jacket and jeans worn by model Claudia Schiffer on a beach in the Caribbean may seem a long way from the reality of most people's lives, but from it we can learn that: (a) beach wear may be more elegant if you're covered up; (b) a structured jacket can be made to look casual.

● Look for basic items that reappear season after season, such as blazers, classic trousers, white shirts, bodies and leggings.

● Don't just look at the pictures; read the text, captions and headings, which will spell out points you may have missed. It's not unusual for fashion to reflect the way women are feeling about themselves at a given time—their priorities, their needs, their hopes and their frustrations. Copy writers make it their job to extract new attitudes and choose their words carefully.

OTHER POINTS OF REFERENCE

All good newspapers have a regular fashion column. They're great for immediate reports from the runways, and often run extra fashion pages during the collections. Outside the collections, though, frantic deadlines and newspaper reproduction can cramp their style visually. The advantage of newspapers is that their journalists usually write about the current season, which will jog your memory about what you discovered in magazines.

Foreign glossies also make for good reference material, especially some French, Italian and American ones. The stockists, of course, will have little relevance, but the extra images can only heighten your awareness of the season's mood. Plus, they prove that the silhouettes and moods you've already spotted can be interpreted by a different selection of clothes, which is a lesson you can apply to your own wardrobe. Flicking through back copies of magazines also has worth, because out-dated concepts stand out a mile. You'll find true classic elements don't actually change too much, but the way they're styled may have undergone a total transformation: it is instructive to compare the length of skirt showing below a blazer, the different heights of shoes, the hair, the location and accessories.

Pay designer shops a visit to see how an item you've seen in a magazine actually looks on the hanger. Feel it, really get to grips with the type of fabric, cut and subtle details you'll be looking for. Try it on to see if it's going to be a look that's suitable for you and judge how it would work with your existing clothes. The silence and the clothes hanging up like prize exhibits can make designer shops seem intimidating, but you're entitled to look round with no obligation to buy. If you really can't face them, a morning spent window shopping is the next best thing.

Now set yourself a test: notice what other people wear—in the street, at parties, on television. Ask yourself why you love or dislike what they have on and make a mental note of how you would change things.

Right *The elegance of tall slender Egyptian columns underlines the mood of a statuesque dress.*